Within The Creases

A. C. French

BookLeaf
Publishing

India | USA | UK

Presentation by *BookLeaf Publishing*

Web: www.bookleafpub.com

E-mail: info@bookleafpub.com

ISBN : 9789358362213

First edition 2021

The Fall From Grace

She bites her lips and they start to
bleed,
Dripping past chipped nails and on white
linen sheets.
The window has been left open and the
rain has flooded in,
The pages of the book next to it read
nothing but ruin.
The tea has turned cold in the China
cup
Which is covered in ivy and
forget-me-nots.

She sipped from it last summer in a field
full of colour,
Under a parasol, eating strawberries
and reading a book from hermother.

Her nails, all polished diamonds,
matched the dainty ring
That wrapped around her tiny finger as
a promise for something.
Her lips were like pink roses, so smooth
and so plush,
Forever tarnished from the kiss of her
recent love.

But affairs of the heart can get tangled in
life's web
And not every story containing love has
a happy end.
Word spread like pollen and seeds of
scandal grew,
Strangling all freedom so no light could
shine through.
Like a moth she stayed by the flame for
too long

And when she returned from the fields,
the ring on her finger was gone.
The neighbourhood whispered though
the truth was disguised
And they wrapped her in shame even
when they heard her cry.

How poetic is the fall from grace,
A hopeless romantic hiding her face.
Scared to dream again and fall from the
stage,
The sun has set on her golden age.
But in the bleakness of the night,
A phoenix takes its first flight.
A mythical being spreading fiery wings,
The creature of the sun and new
beginnings.

Fish Bowls

We all live in fish bowls.
Will we sink or will we float?

They pucker their fish lips as if that's
how they breathe,
They stare with wide eyes as if they
struggle to see.
They drop open their empty, gaping
mouths,
But no valuable sound ever flows out.
All are synchronized, as if purposely
cloned,
Even the water they float in isn't their
own.

And yet people always flock around their
bowls.

They praise and reward them by double
tapping on their walls.
They throw in yachts overflowing with
rich champagne,
Then scroll along the row and do it all
again.
The fish only care for the price of their
scales.
They're worth nothing at all.
Nothing to us.

We poured our own water from our
differentfountains.
We love, we cry, we climb the tallest
mountains.
Around our bowls we dance in the
brightest of colours.
Our incandescent souls glow.
We do it for the spark that ignites a
passion,

A feeling worth more than beauty or
fashion.

And yet they laugh and spit in our bowls.
They tie doubt and hate and fear around
our ankles,
Watching with green eyes as we sink
and struggle.
If we're strong enough we will survive; if
we're weak we will crumble.
But the ruins will be majestic.
Everyone will remember us as they
stare into the glass,
Our stories won't be forgotten unlike the
clones they pass.

We all live in fish bowls.
Will you sink or will you float?

Water Marks

Rain leaves its mark on pavements.
It runs down drains, down windows,
down faces.
We attempt to outrun it but it always
catches us with dark smudges under our
eyes.

We catch our breath under porches,
between laughs and pauses,
as we take in the petrichor scent.
It reminds me of a well used book, full of
adventure and new beginnings, waiting
to be read again.

Soaking through our clothes, hands
cold, as it seeps into skin like sin.
And it always wins.

The source of life revives our souls,
buried in the dry cracks of our palms.
Just like that we're leaping and dancing,
as if awoken by some alarm.

The body aches under hazy light as
water drips through hair and down
closed eyes.
Amid the steam and the blushed
cheeks, the coursing water feels like
luxury.
The mind is still, no concerns or cares
for details, just resting in the warmth.
Not happy, not sad,
not scared, not fearless.
Just still in the moment as if captured on
camera.

Superglue

I tried to fix you but you kept pulling
yourself apart.
So to fill the gaps I gave you a piece of
my heart.
I had no idea it would start a war, a
burning rage of passion that left me
breathless and stained to the bone.
What was the lesson?
Yes, my optimism still remains,
Like a reminder that the good people
feel the most pain.
I care, I care, I care until it destroys me,
until I
I shut down and need new batteries.
Until someone plugs me in to a new love
charge
And then it happens again and I fall
apart.

Did my cracks show from the others I
tried to fix?
They say words hurt less than stones
and sticks but that cliche doesn't work.
When your sweet sparks leave your lips,
they make my ears bleed and burn.

I offered out a hand and you cut it off
with a smile.

Quick! I need some super glue because
I broke my back in two bending all of my
rules for you.
But nobody comes to pick up my lifeless
body,
Nobody stops, cares or worries.
Maybe it's because I don't cry for help,
I guess I'll just have to mend myself.

Miracle String

I've heard we're made of stars,
Some miracle string connecting us to
the universe.
One tiny snap would bring everything
crashing down,
But for millions of years we've stayed
tied together.
Planets align, the sun shines, nature
blasts it's mighty roar and here we are
so intricately designed.

Aren't we just insignificant organisms
floating around in the grand stadium of
existence?
No.
We are impossible.
A single speck of magic transformed
nothing into everything,

Blooming like a rose, and like pollen
we're at it's centre.
We love, we inspire, we struggle, we
strive, we feel the deepest emotions and
forever question why,
But we'll never receive the answers.
Our lives are supposed to be surprising
twists and turns, rises and falls across
the pages laid out before us.
Our future is always unexpected, even if
planned to the atom,
Our pages are creased with our past.

I've heard that most of the ocean is still
a mystery.
Anything could inhibit the Prussian blue
depths, untouched by humankind's
maddening hands.
We see thousands of shoals and
schools swish by,

Each pattern and colour is so flawlessly
carved but in time they may fade away.
Fade like the shore melting into waves.
The sculpted beauty of nature is fragile
and its leaves crumble between our
fingertips.

Nothing insignificant is trusted with the
amount of power we hold within us.
Homes can be built through the love in
our hearts,
Mountains can be conquered through
the strength of our minds,
And worlds can be constructed through
our words.
Do you see?
Life itself is ephemeral,
But the creases we make in the
universe are eternal.

I've heard that we're the product of
accidents with every detail coming down
to chance.
The elements are tied up perfectly with
not a hair out of place.
Even the birds, the trees, the clouds the
seas sit in their golden frame,
As if painted by Monet.
But like every masterpiece, the critics
come and try to tear it down.
They don't see what lays before them,
The brush strokes of heaven.

The single thread from the beginning
leads to you, right here and now.
You could be anywhere across the
universe but you've wound up reading
this somehow.
The miracle string that lead you through
your life will guide you through the dark,

Until one day the curtain falls and you're

reunited with the stars.

Love-Lies-Bleeding

The gardens of Château de Villandry
were in full bloom as he ran to catch her,
The whole of the land heard her squeals
of laughter.
Their clandestine meetings were
unknown to all,
And they would lay in the clearing
For hours next to the
Love-Lies-Bleeding,
Until the starry nightfall.

Illicit kisses tattooed his lips in berry red,
"I'll never love another while I'm alive
And I'll never love another when I'm
dead,"
He said.
She danced with him in the summer
showers,

Ran her fingers through his chestnut
hair,
They knew they could never marry but
neither of them cared.
"Charlotte please be careful,
No one must know what we do,"
He whispered as he was just a gardener
And she was the daughter of the duke.
Charlotte laughed with crystal eyes and
twirled the locket around her neck,
She promised not to tell another soul
even with her final breath.

One night he climbed the ladder of ivy
leading to her window,
And she opened up to her surreptitious
lover only visible by the moon's glow.
His hands moved down her body as if in
time with a song,

And both their hearts chimed together

as if they made up one.

He craved for her like sugar,

Though he could never give her gold,

And he climbed back down the ivy

before the August sun rose.

Letters sealed with blood red wax

flowed to and from her chambers,

Charlotte indulged in every desperate

word,

And their contents of liaison.

She kept their secret though she feared

it would bring her name dishonour,

If the scent broke loose from grip,

It would wake the green eyed monster.

Charlotte had wealthy admirers who

swarmed and flashed their pearly fangs,

But neither set her soul ablaze

Or, when it rained, asked her to dance.
One man tried to capture her,
But his slyness made her shudder,
And when she didn't accept his hand he
knew it belonged to another.

The man was devoured in stubborn
madness,
He would not stop until Charlotte was
his wife,
So he intercepted all her letters and
followed her at night.
She glided out the grand stone walls to
her midnight meeting,
The man slinked in the shadows,
And hid behind the Love-Lies-Bleeding.
He saw his opponent and fixed him to a
target in his mind,
Acquiring a crafty plan to win Charlotte
as his prize.

After days of no encounter,

Charlotte's lover received a letter.

He opened the red wax seal,

And ran to the garden to meet her.

The golden hour of sunset scattered

beams all around,

When he reached the clearing he found

her locket on the ground.

Summer breeze cooled his warm skin

As he scanned the garden for his love,

But his heart paused sharply when he

saw the man behind the cluster of

foxglove.

He knew that the man had come for

him,

But he yelled for Charlotte all the same.

She did not hear his cry as she had

been concealed from the game.

Her lover stood in a trance as if time
was not his master,
He begged his feet to run away but they
did not give an answer.
The arrow was released and cut through
the air's tide,
And like a silent magnet it struck deep
into his side.
He stumbled back in disbelief as the
man ran out of sight,
Then to his knees he crumbled down
still clutching the locket tight.
Blood tapped at the ground below as he
laid back in agony,
His tears burned down his cheeks like
the ending of a tragedy.
After a final look at the setting sun,
He closed his eyes as if sleeping,
He laid there as he had before next to
the Love-Lies-Bleeding.

The gardens of Château de Villandry

were silent as she ran to find him.

She collapsed down by his side,

As the whole land heard her crying.

Her arms that wrapped around him were

stained a potent red,

"I'll never love another while I'm alive

And I'll never love another when I'm

dead,"

She cried.

Charlotte didn't want to keep the secret

anymore.

She laid with him in the clearing,

Next to the Love-Lies-Bleeding,

Until the starry nightfall.

Alisha

We used to roller skate around the park,

Scrape our knees,

Be in before dark.

We ate ice creams that stained our lips

bright blue,

I had other friends,

But none were like you.

Sleepovers and karaoke,

Messy painted toes.

I ate too many chocolate strawberries,

You watched all the Disney shows.

We were always polar opposites except

for four blue eyes,

You've always been much tidier than

me,

We're like sugar and spice.

We walked to school everyday,

And sometimes ran home in the rain.
Eating pizza in your front garden,
when summer finally came.
Through every success and every
failure,
Every spark of laughter and every tear,
We've been through it all together
And we will throughout the years.
When the monsters came and knocked
you down,
I stood and fought them all,
And when I needed answers or a place
for peace,
It was always you I would call.

Our memories will always stick with me,
Tattooed into my mind,
The ink will never fade or smudge
Because our friendship will never die.
I know we're getting older,

And our paths may turn separate ways.

But just remember in the story of my life,

Your name is on every page.

I used to be…

I used to be a princess.

I went to balls in long hooped dresses

And dance all night long with princes.

I was rescued from a tall stone tower

And lived happily ever after.

I used to be a wizard.

I casted spells and flew around

Turning people into frogs.

I fought off all the evil beings,

And I was the best wizard there ever

was.

I used to be a scientist.

I spent all day up in my lab,

Mixing chemicals and dissecting plants.

Coming up with big experiments,

I was clever and I was mad.

I used to be a chef.

I owned a big restaurant

And made the best dishes in the city.

Pasta, chicken, pizza, cake

Anything you wanted,

I put it on your plate.

I used to be a child.

Big dreams and big wishes,

My imagination was wild.

I'd make islands out of blankets,

And forts out of pillows.

I danced wherever I went,

And make stories out of shadows.

Now I sit at a work desk,

Wondering when it all stopped.

We could do anything in the world,

And we treasured everything we got.

Adults seem to forget the magic
moments in the little things,
The specks of kindness, friendship,
happiness
That gives us strength to spread our
wings.

Within the creases

Like the creases in your favourite shirt,
The creases of your life tell the story of
your past.
Indentations that are drawn across the
frangible skin of your palms.

The folds of pain,

The gaps of love,

The lines of age.

We tread lightly on the tightropes
between them,
Praying to vanity that they don't drag us
down.
The creases are said to be monsters.

So people hide them away in a locked
draw,
Behind clothes and makeup and doctor
receipts,

Out of sight but never really out of mind.

Why keep the door locked?

Your life should be celebrated.
You don't have to be a genius, or a
healer, or speak the loudest to matter.
Every crease echoes memories,
The intricate cracks create gateways to
your identity
And allow your soul to shine through.

Cherry

She is a goddess,
Sculpted from an angelic mould and
dipped in rich, warm heaven.

A photo wouldn't capture all her streams
of beauty,
Even da Vinci's brush wouldn't graze the
surface of her grandeur.

Auburn curls bounce past her shoulders,
Even glossier than her lips,
And freckles outline her big bronze eyes
like scattered shards of glitter.

I've never seen eyes like hers before,
They charm you in an instant glance.

She could be on the cover of vogue,

Her clothes envelope around her body
in a vintage yet timeless fashion.
Like a lion in her prime she strides
ahead of the sheep.

I love her but I'm not in love with her.
I love the way she smiles with her whole
face when she passes by,
Lighting up the dullest Monday
mornings.
I admire her in all her uniqueness.

With more people like her,
The world would sparkle.

Empowerment

The truth is, I don't feel empowered at
all.
I feel left out, pushed aside, abused,
and small.
The others can fake a smile and walk
around looking confident,
But deep inside I'm sure they've cried
and felt just lost in it -
In all of the words, the phrases, the calls
across the street,
Yes we may wear trousers and make
speeches but is that really equality?
If we still look others in the eye and use
words that imply we are lesser,
Can the future generations really make
society better?
There's goodness flowing from fresh
representation,

But there's no point destroying the tower
if you leave the foundation.

I stand with shaking hands,
My words quake in fear of being
misunderstood.
In fear of being called hysterical,
emotional and wrongfully judged
For just wanting peace.
Even if I never see the day,
There will be silence when we walk the
streets.

We will be seen as equal and strong,
In a society where we can thrive and
feel like we belong
Because, although they don't see it, the
world would shrivel without us.
Without gasoline, what would move the
bus?

I have hope that the clouds of injustice

will clear one day,

whether I'm dead or still alive.

But it all starts within the making of

history today,

Will you pick a side?

The Land Of The Mountains

Cool water flows through the land of the
mountains-
the exposed, beating heart of nature.
Travellers have tread through its mossy
valleys,
Poets have gazed upon the bracken
backs of the sleeping giants,
And flocks have grazed on the multitude
of forbs they carry.

And here I stand looking over it all.

The rise and fall of nature's heartbeat,
stretches out across the ancient scroll.

It's perpetual artistry is illustrated with
tiny cracks and creases,

All arteries building together to create a
regal sculpture.

Humankind's feeble structures bow
before it in fear.
The fear that something this grand and
more powerful than them exists,
And it consumes their own existence.

The hand of time has not touched the
land of the mountains,
It cannot reach through the maze of
undergrowth which protects the heart
from the wrinkles of age.

Poets have attempted to record the
essence,
Flowing from each vein.
But the current is too strong for anyone
to truly capture its greatness.

The glory shines like a beacon

throughout the villages and the towns,

As if a reminder that no hand crafted

object could ever compete.

And in the gallery of the universe,

No matter how simple things appear,

The unrefined sources leave the most

permanent and memorable footprints.

Inner Child

I still make snowmen when it snows,

Catch icy flakes on my nose,

Sledging down the hill as fast as my little

board can go.

I smell all the festive candles,

Reminding me of Christmas past.

I hang up stockings,

Leave out mince pies

And I wish the holidays could last.

I eat men made from gingerbread

And sing carols,

Whilst wearing tinsel and a Santa hat

onmy head.

Spring thaws the frosty fields,

And flower heads poke up.

I skip past in a long dress,

Looking for clovers to test my luck.

I hunt for chocolate eggs,

don't care how much I eat,

Gaze at all the baby lambs

And climb the tallest trees.

When the rain bursts from the fluffy

clouds,

I grab my wellies and run out.

I laugh and jump around with my hair

dripping wet,

But I don't mind because I take every

chance to dance I get.

Summer's made for water fights,

Balloons smack into hot skin.

Racing to the ice cream van,

I love it because I always win.

I still make sandcastles at the beach,

And swim until I can see the fish.

Practice handstands and cartwheels,

Catching fairies to make a wish.

I collect all the daisies to make the
longestchain,
Picnics under a golden sun,
I sleep then do it all again.

Autumn paints the leaves a crimson
brown
I still stamp on the crunchiest,
And love watching them fall to the
ground.
Sparklers warm my heart with delight,
While I watch fireworks burst into the
night.
Marshmallows swim in hot, sweet
chocolate,
Poured in a cup wrapped in woolly
gloves.
Crisp morning air on my bare rosy
cheeks,

The dwindling cinnamon scent is
something I still love.
I still dress up in black with a witches
hat,
Carrying a cauldron with enough sugar
to turn any child mad.

With each year and new moon and
setting of the sun,
We get older and wiser but have a lot
less fun.
Like a child finds joy with each seasonal
change,
We should appreciate that zest for life is
not limited to age.
Now replaying all the scenes from our
recorded past,
There's no doubt our character has
changed as our roles never last.

But no knowledge or power nor strength

nor time,

Is ever equal to that tape that keeps our

inner child alive.

Ignorance Is Bliss

What you don't know can't hurt you,
That's how the saying goes.

I agree.

I turn off the news,
I can't read the comments anymore.
I feel immense pain standing in their
shoes,
But is it weak to close the door?

Tears of fire burn down my face,
Make it stop.
I turn around and see the strings of
privilege that I've got,
But for others they're broken and
twisted.
The weight of inequity is crushing,

And I'm not even the one carrying it.

There's not a home for some,
There's not a side for some,
There's not a choice for some
And some just lose it all.

There's so much hate for some,
There's so much pain for some,
There's so much rain for some
And some have to take it all.

Ignorance is bliss,
Just like when you were a kid,
In a world where there's no hate or
violence or judging stares.
Where the only evil that exists are the
villains in the comics.
You can just close the cover and turn off
the light without being too scared .

No one else seems to care that much,
Or panic when there's waves crashing at
society's walls.
A historical tsunami of oppression
swallowing all the goodness,
But no one seems to notice at all.

And I'm drowning in it.

I retreat to my bubble once again,
Where for just a few moments I can
pretend that no one is dying.
There's no hate, no children crying,
No pain, no wars that need fighting.
You can call me delusional and tell me
to stop lying,
But I know the truth.
I'm just hiding for a while,

Because I've always found my

imagination more enjoyable than reality.

And what you don't know can't hurt you.

Pandemic

Eyes smile over blue masks,
They all share the same drained out
hollowness.

Cracked skin around the knuckles,
They've been scrubbed at every
entrance.

Bruises and red traces around faces,
They've been fighting for life,
But there's more and more cases.
They're outnumbered, cornered,
Surrounded by all sides.
But they still throw their tools,
They still try to conquer death,
They won't give up and hide.

Then there are those who simply don't
care.
They know that people are dying,
They know that people are fighting,
But they only care if they're the ones
surviving.
There is a cruel line between the right
thing and
"What's the point?"
This line shows us the chain that binds
us all together,
We don't see it at first,
But it's always there clanking as we
trudge through life.
If one person pulls too hard,
Another will fall to the ground.

So the reason people are dying must be
because people aren't trying,

And the ones who are, are hidden out of
the scene.
Like a puppet master in charge of the
strings.

We wait in our homes,
Video calls on phones,
Longing for our friends and family,
But we do as we're told.
Because we know the consequences
our actions have,
So we keep our distance.

We wear a mask.

Intertwined

Four starry eyes,
A mercurial high.

Hunger for a heart race,
Hand on my thigh.

Warm breath clinging to my neck,
Lips of desire.

I want more each time,
Two bodies on fire.

Pull away like the tide,
I pull back in like a wave.

Skin bound to skin
No time to waste.

Two stars collide,

It ripples through space.

The film just keeps running,

No pause or delays.

Minds in deep slumber,

But our passion is awake.

Our words could not describe,

So our lips send the message.

Hands smooth over my creases,

Mending all my ripped edges.

Running

gotta run

gotta run

gotta let it all out

i'm burning up the runway

gotta fight

gotta fight

gotta stamp the ground

i'm a phoenix taking flight

when they claw at my peace

and bite at my words

they colour me red

now i'm screaming at the moon

in an open field in the middle of the night

the shade of blue

shines through my bones and sets my

soul alight

i let it all out

don't care if the wolves howl

i let it all out

nothing can hold me back now

when they tear down my castle

and destroy the home i made

i run into the field so i can escape.

letting the wolves run free without a fight

letting it all burst out into the night

like phoenix taking flight.

Shades of Wine (part 1)

A pink sunrise lights up Camden Street,
5 AM.
Darcie staggers on her tiptoes,
Passing silent houses,
Stilettos in hand.

Smudges of mascara plaster her under
eyes,
Black hair escapes from the last
remaining pin.
A dress torn at the end hangs from her
shoulders,
No repairs could ever revive it.

She left the red house alone,
Without the wine she had brought the
night before,

Without her dignity she had always
worn.
The bruises around her neck are now
turning purple,
The slash across her arm is now dried,
And the streets are empty except for
another soul passing by.

Darcie recognises Penny from the
photographs.
Her blonde hair pinned up in neat curls,
Makeup fixed to her smooth skin,
Cherry lips drawn in velvet,
Appearing flawless even in the early
hours.
She glides past in a flurry of sweet
perfume,
Unaware of Darcie's existence.

Darcie glares at the blood lining,

Buried in her fingernails.

She reaches the street sign,

Marking the end.

Before she turns the corner she peers

over her shoulder,

The red house faintly in view,

With Penny's poison scream penetrating

through its walls

Shades of Wine (part 2)

Crimson stained hands now crimson
stained floor.
Droplets plummet to the ground,
A meteor shower striking the bathroom
tiles.
A kitchen knife balances on the side of
the sink,
It's murderous blade winking cunningly
in the spotlight.

Merlot had been poured into new
glasses,
Some had spilled over in a sudden fever
and stained the white rug.
Penny's husband was known for
drinking too much,
But she did not expect the bottom of the
bottle to drive a knife into his chest.

Penny sinks to the ground eyes fixed on
the lifeless body,
In the absence of tears.
A loveless marriage leaves holes that
others swoop in to fill,
And she has known of her husband's
infidelity,
But money is almost as complicated as
the heart.

The phone is held up to her crystal
pierced ear,
As Penny tries to round up the suspects
in her mind.
Pink gloss around the rim of a glass
reads the killer as a woman,
The cheap bottle describes her as
young.

Captivating evidence confirms her
suspicions.
She picks up a black hair pin,
Something she would never wear,
Carelessly thrown behind the soap tray.

Sirens enclose the red house.
Penny stands on the front door steps,
Blood still smeared on her hands.
And through the swarms of police and
ambulances,
As if everything else had slowed for just
this moment,
Across the street,
Penny's eyes meet with Darcie's for the
first time.

Why I Cry

I sometimes cry at the sky,
Thanking God that I have found my best
friend in this lifetime.
She's as rare as a total eclipse,

The planets aligning,

Purple carrots.

Soul completion is hard to obtain when
you're young.
But there is no other wonder in time,

No amount of stars that fill the night,
That comes close to the fullness of my
heart.

I sometimes cry at the sky,

I care so much for people I'll never meet
so some say I've lost my mind.
I hear their hearts screaming to be
protected,
Each one is so rare in colour and
character,
But each one is equal in worth.

I think the world has lost its mind.
Its population is deaf to the scraping
blade of injustice,

It's crippling.

I sometimes cry at the sky,
The passion within me spills through the
creases.

The stories I am yet to tell,

The messages I am yet to convey,

The seeds of legacy I am yet to scatter.

The cards will reveal new flowers,
With new seasons of challenges,
And I will care for them all until they
grow into blessings.
Words are said to be the deadliest
weapon,
But I intend to use them to paint the
most captivating sunsets.